VICTORIA AND ALBERT MUSEUM

EARLY RAILWAY PRINTS

From the collection of Mr and Mrs M G Powell

Michael Darby

LONDON: HER MAJESTY'S STATIONERY OFFICE

ISBN 0 11 290321 5

FOREWORD

The exhibition which this booklet originally accompanied
was made possible through the willingness of Mr and Mrs
Michael Powell to put at the disposal of the Department
of Prints and Drawings their large collection of railway
prints, and the Museum was much indebted to them for
this most generous action. Their collection conveys a
remarkably clear record of early railway development in
particular, and it is that aspect which has been emphasised
in the present publication. These prints impart both the
excitement the artists felt at the unprecedented scale of
the engineering works called forth by the Railway Age and
their sense of the social revolution which this technological
advance was to bring about.

Michael Darby, who has compiled the catalogue and
written the introduction, wishes to express his gratitude to
Lt.-Col. T. M. Simmons, now retired from the staff of the
Science Museum, for making his great knowledge on all
matters connected with railways available to him whenever he needed assistance.

C. M. KAUFFMANN
Keeper
Department of Prints, Drawings, Photographs & Paintings

First the shrill whistle, then the distant roar,
The Ascending cloud of steam, the gleaming brass,
The mighty moving arm; and on amain
The mass comes thundering like an avalanche o'er
The quaking earth; a thousand faces pass—
A moment, and are gone. Like whirlwind sprites,
Scarce seen; so much the roaring speed benights
All sense and recognition for a while;
A little space, a minute, and a mile.
Then look again, how swift it journeys on;
Away, away, along the horizon
Like drifted cloud, to its determined place;
Power, speed, and distance melting into space.

The Pleasures of the Rail-Road.___ Cought in the Railway!

Railways provided a constant source of material for caricaturists.
This print was one of a series produced after the opening of the Liverpool and Manchester Railway in 1830.

INTRODUCTION

WHEN GEORGE STEPHENSON took Fanny Kemble for a ride on the 'Rocket' she was enthralled by 'the magical machine with the flying white breath' which sped her at more than twenty miles an hour between 'great masses of stone . . . cut asunder to allow our passage . . . far below the surface of the earth . . . no fairy tale was ever half so wonderful'. She stood with her bonnet off and felt as if she were flying 'you cannot conceive what that sensation of cutting the air was'. Her delight in these new and invigorating phenomena was not apparently shared by Queen Victoria, who was more conscious of the convenience of the railway, writing after her first journey, from London to Windsor in 1842, that it had taken 'half an hour free from dust and crowd and heat and I am quite charmed with it'. Their wonder at the almost mystical quality of contemporary technical and scientific achievement as manifested in the railway undoubtedly reflected a widespread attitude. Many of the artists who drew the first stations, viaducts and bridges allowed their subjects to harmonise so successfully with the landscape that they do not appear to be the products of an industrial revolution but the result of a process of natural selection. Few had seriously considered the constructional, economic and other problems of building and running the railways, and consequently give little indication of the cost in terms of human skill and labour. The change in what George Eliot called the 'speech' of the landscape—'the hills are cut through or the breaches between them spanned, we choose our level, and the white steam-pennon flies along it'—did not apparently concern them.

One railway artist in particular, however, John Cooke Bourne the author of *Drawings of the London and Birmingham Railway* (1839) and *The History and Description of the Great Western Railway* (1846), could accept the lines, forms and proportions of modern technology at face value while many of his contemporaries struggled to come to terms with the aesthetic problem posed by the fact that mechanism lacked elegance of line and, more importantly, with the moral issue of its inhumanity. The locomotive had superhuman strength without human form, although it could not operate without human guidance. John Martin depicted a train in his *Last Judgement* but only to carry the damned to Hell in third class carriages. To accept these new forms was to reject the idealistic teaching of academicism

in favour of what Victor Hugo termed 'le caractéristique', even though that meant studying 'le vulgaire et le trivial'. Thus, Bourne could depict the Kilsby tunnel with water seeping through the floor while workmen labour with shovels, and horses, used to drag away the rubble, stand exhausted.

The acceptance of these characteristic and specific qualities heralded the era of documentary illustration and of a new generation of artists which sprang up to meet the demand for railway and other views. Bourne, and his contemporary Thomas Talbot Bury, the author of volumes on the London and Birmingham, and Liverpool and Manchester Railways, and architect of many buildings in the south of England, were joined by others. Among them were the self-taught landscape and animal painter Arthur Fitzwilliam Tait, whose *Views on the Manchester and Leeds Railway* was published in 1845; the marine artist J. W. Carmichael; T. M. Richardson and his five sons; George Hawkins; and numerous less well known local artists.

Spectacular engineering projects have always stirred the public imagination beyond its enthusiasm for more general technological progress, and prints of these subjects were always popular, regardless of their aesthetic merit or their ability, by depicting stages of construction, to make comprehensible that which had seemed impossible. Thus, numerous views were made by many different artists of Brunel's bridge at Saltash, of Stephenson's Britannia bridge over the Menai Straits, and of similar large undertakings. The strictly utilitarian character of engineering designs such as these could be seen to produce models of form perfectly adapted to function, and consequently beautiful. Writing in his *Entretiens sur l'architecture* in 1863, Viollet le Duc found in the locomotive the same answer to the problem of style which some architects had seen in Paxton's iron and glass Crystal Palace, 'pour tout le monde, la locomotive . . . a sa physionomie qui en fait une création à part. Rien n'indique mieux que ces lourdes machines roulantes la force domptée; ses mouvements sont doux ou terribles, elle s'avance avec une farouche indépendance ou semble frémir d'impatience sous la main de ce petit homme qui la lance ou l'arrête à son gré. La locomotive est presque un être, et sa forme extérieure n'est que l'expression de sa puissance. Une locomotive donc a du style'.

Many of the issues which so concerned these artists were, in fact, at the heart of the French Romantic Revolution of 1830, and the various utopian socialist groups which sprang up at that time in both France and England sought not just to come to terms with technology but to find a compromise between art and industry. Their belief in great public works inevitably attracted engineers. Eugène Flachat, the builder of France's first railway in 1837, and Michel Chevalier, who in 1833–35 visited America on behalf of the French government to study the railway system there, were both followers of Henri de Saint-Simon, the radical philosopher who expounded a doctrine of individual freedom through scientific and industrial development. Soon Carlyle could see 'Indications ... in other countries and in our own, signs infinitely cheering to us, that mechanism is not always to be our hard task master, but one day to be our pliant, all-ministering servant'; and later Dr Arnold on watching a train on the Rugby line remarked 'I rejoice to see it, and think that feudality is gone forever. It is so great a blessing to think that any one evil is really extinct'.

The social effects of railway development were widely publicised by writers and cartoonists. As early as 1823 Walter Scott wrote to Joanna Baillie about 'the increasing powers of steam which, like you, I look on half-proud, half-sad, half-angry, and half-pleased in doing so much for the commercial world promise something also for the sociable'. He could look forward to a time when the picturesque scenery depicted in so many early nineteenth century travel books could be experienced in reality, when sea-side holidays would be available to all, and when Hampstead and Abbotsford would be within the distance of ' "Will you dine with us quietly tomorrow?" '. But the passing of the horse and carriage, and of the deliberation which preceded the journey and enjoyable interludes which accompanied it, for the spontaneity and conventional mobility of modern travel, was not to everyone's taste. Ruskin wrote in the *Stones of Venice* (1853) 'In the olden days of travelling, now to return no more, in which distance could not be vanquished without toil, but in which that toil was rewarded, partly by the power of deliberate survey of the countries through which the journey lay, and partly by the happiness of the evening hours, when from the top of the last hill he had surmounted, the traveller beheld the

quiet village where he was to rest, scattered among the meadow beside its valley stream; or, from the long-hoped-for turn in the dusty perspective of the causeway, saw for the first time, the towers of some famed city, faint in the rays of sunset-hours of peaceful and thoughtful pleasure, for which the rush of the arrival in the railway station is perhaps not always, or to all men, an equivalent,—in those days, I say, when there was something more to be anticipated and remembered in the first aspect of each successive halting-place, than a new arrangement of glass roofing and iron girder'.

Some critics attacked the noise and smoke, and particularly the damage to the environment caused by the railways. 'Is there no nook of English ground secure from rash assault?' asked Wordsworth when he heard of the projected line through the Lake District. Others worried about the dangers of travelling at high speed—no human being could breathe at more than sixty miles an hour—of being run over, blown-up, or simply of falling from the carriages. 'Does anybody mean to say' asked *John Bull* in 1835 'that decent people, passengers who would use their own carriages, and are accustomed to their own comforts,

would consent to be hurried along through the air upon a railroad, from which, had a lazy schoolboy left a marble, or a wicked one a stone, they would be pitched off their perilous track into the valley beneath; or is it to be imagined that women, who may like the fun of being whirled away on a party of pleasure for an hour to see a sight, would endure the fatigue, and misery, and danger, not only to themselves, but their children and families, of being dragged through the air at the rate of twenty miles an hour, all their lives being at the mercy of a tin pipe, or a copper boiler, or the accidental dropping of a pebble on the line of way?' Scorn was poured upon the railway navvies who sometimes wrought havoc in the areas in which they were employed, stealing, damaging property, and carrying off other men's wives; but who themselves had good reason to complain about often appalling working conditions, insanitary accommodation, low wages and the heavy casualties they suffered in accidents.

Cartoonists revelled in the opportunities which these themes provided. One depicted Colonel Sibthorp MP, an opponent of the railways, charging on horseback with primitive lance raised hopelessly against a speeding loco-

motive; another, a family being literally eaten alive by the railway monster—'I come to dine, I come to sup, I come I come—to eat you up!!'—and another, two heedless engine drivers reclining in comfort while their locomotive runs down all who stand in its path. *Punch* even reflected on a railway 'from London to Canton, passing through the centre of the globe', upon a terminus 'on the present site of St. Paul's Cathedral, London, which for the purposes of this undertaking, is to be pulled down', and upon a railway underneath London.

But however much one regretted the passing of the horse and carriage, and idealised the way of life which they represented, the benefits offered by the railways were far too compelling to be ignored. After 27 September 1825, when, amid enormous excitement, Stephenson's 'Locomotion' successfully hauled the first train from Shildon to Stockton on the Stockton and Darlington Railway the rapid development of other lines was assured. Even at that time the Liverpool and Manchester Railway was sufficiently advanced for the thirteenth toast after the celebratory dinner in Stockton Town Hall to be drunk to its 'success', the Bill for the Canterbury and Whitstable Railway had been passed, and the London and Birmingham Railway Company had been formed.

What has often been described as 'railway mania' ensued. Parliament was pressed with hundreds of schemes for new lines; numerous amateur civil engineers sprang up, abandoning jobs as clerks, apprentices, merchants, army officers and tradesmen; and thousands made and lost fortunes investing in the new companies. Locomotives even engaged in trials of strength to prove the claims of rival companies. 'The engine of the Shrewsbury and Birmingham slowly advanced in spite of the red flags hoisted, and amidst the cheers and shouts of the assembled multitude, butted against that of the London and North Western'. Different companies constructed lines through the same districts. 'Look at the vicinity of London', asked the *Athenaeum* in 1843, 'two railways—the Northern and Eastern, and the Eastern Counties, to Cambridge and to Colchester—are carried in the same district; both are unsuccessful—one might have served the purposes of both, and perhaps neither is the line that should have been adopted. At all events one of the two is useless—total loss, say £1,000,000. When going north, we have two lines

parallel with each other, the Birmingham and Derby, and the Midland Counties, the latter of which should never have existed—total loss, £1,000,000. Then the Chester and Crew, Manchester and Crewe, and Newton and Crewe . . . '. The problems posed by these unneccessary lines were not entirely solved until the present century when, as part of the cuts proposed by Lord Beeching, and others, many were closed. Now it is the main lines alone which are being developed, not for steam, or even diesel, but for electric trains.

'The distant roar, the ascending cloud of steam, the gleaming brass [and] the mighty moving arm' remain little more than nostalgic memories. The modern locomotive moves quietly and effortlessly along the track, an occasional flash of blue light from the thin wires overhead is all that indicates that great power is involved. Unlike the steam locomotive it cannot be seen to be working, the forces which drive it can only be imagined. The contemporary artist, confronted with such extremely sophisticated mechanisms, involving processes and theories which he cannot hope to understand, has had to adopt a more philosophical approach to his work than that of his nineteenth century counterpart. Straightforward representations no longer served his purpose, and consequently the intellectual demands on the beholder of his pictures became correspondingly greater. John Bourne and Thomas Talbot Bury and their contemporaries needed no more than their precise vision and accurate draughtsmanship to adequately express the excitement and dynamism of the new industrial age in which they lived.

Prior Park the Seat of Ralph Allen Esqr. near Bath

Lettered with title in English and French and Drawn from Mr Allen's Road. Ant: Walker Sculpt. Printed for R. Wilkinson, No. 58 Cornhill, London.
Engraving, coloured by hand
$11\frac{1}{8}$ in × $17\frac{1}{4}$ in (28·3 cm × 43·7 cm)

Several wooden wagonways, the forerunners of later iron railways, had been constructed by the beginning of the eighteenth century, in Shropshire and other northern mining centres, to facilitate the removal of coal and ironstone from quarries. It was apparently these that inspired Ralph Allen, the Post Office reformer, to employ John Padmore to construct for him in 1731 a similar wagonway from Combe Down, where he had begun quarrying Bath stone, past his mansion at Prior Park, to the waiting barges on the River Avon. Many contemporary descriptions of Bath mention the railway. John Evelyn, great-grandson of the diarist, wrote to his father in 1738 explaining how the stones were guided along the incline, descending five hundred feet from the quarry, 'in a very clever manner down to ye town upon carriages with low broad wheels, covered with iron, which run upon a wooden frame made ye length of ye hill, so that when ye machine is sett agoing it runs down ye hill without any help, only one man behind to steer it, & in this manner above three hundred Tunn of stones are carrid down at one load'. Like Defoe in his *Tour Thro the Whole Island of Great Britain* (1762) Evelyn exaggerated the quantity of stone carried, although the wagons could apparently transport several blocks of four tons each.

After Allen's death in 1764 the railway was abandoned, and by 1788 the Reverend S. Shaw reported that horse drawn transport was being used instead, 'to the detriment of the roads and the inconvenience of travellers'.

Canterbury and Whitstable Railway
Opening Day

Signed in ink Geo. Robt. Stephenson.
Lettered View of the Canterbury and Whitstable Railway from over the tunnel taken on the opening day, May 3rd 1830.
T. M. Baynes lithog.. Printed by C. Hullmandel. Canterbury Pubd. by Henry Ward, 14 Sun Street.
Lithograph, coloured by hand
$12\frac{1}{4}$ in $\times$ $16\frac{7}{8}$ in ($31\cdot1$ cm $\times$ $42\cdot8$ cm)

The suggestion that a railway should be built to link Canterbury and Whitstable, a distance of six miles, was made as early as April 1823 by William James, who had previously surveyed the ground. Royal assent to the Bill authorising both the line, and the construction of a harbour at Whitstable, was received on 10 June 1825. James eventually dropped out of the undertaking for various reasons and was replaced by George Stephenson, who delegated first Locke and then John Dixon as engineers. The opening of the railway took place on 3 May 1830, when the locomotive 'Invicta' hauled two trains, made into one of twenty carriages and twelve wagons. After the 'Invicta', which was made by Robert Stephenson and Company and driven during the early days of the line by Edward Fletcher, had been sold nine years later, the line was worked for a short time with stationary engines. Later still, experiments were made on the inclined section of Tyler Hill with an atmospheric system.

The Canterbury and Whitstable Railway was purchased by the South Eastern Railway in 1853 and the line was closed in 1931, but the tunnel at Tyler Hill, half a mile long, remains, as does the 'Invicta', which is now on display at Canterbury.

Stephenson's patent locomotive engine

Lettered Measured & drawn by C. F. Cheffins. Engraved by G. Gladwin. Printed by Gad & Kenningale. John Weale, Architectural Library, 59 High Holborn.
Engraving
$12\frac{1}{4}$ in × $23\frac{3}{4}$ in (30·9 cm × 60·6 cm)
Plate from J. Weale, *Description of the Patent Locomotive Steam Engine*, 1838.

When, in 1804, Richard Trevithick first constructed an engine with wheels which ran successfully on rails and thereby silenced those critics who had said that the wheels would simply slip on the rail and the engine would not move forward, the era of the railway locomotive was born. George Stephenson began experiments at Killingworth with the 'Blucher' in 1814 and from that date made numerous improvements in locomotive design. The firm of Robert Stephenson and Company was formed in 1823, when Robert took over from his father, who was becoming increasingly involved in civil engineering works, responsibility for these experiments. Their early work involved engines for use in collieries, but, after the success of the 'Rocket' at the Rainhill trials in October 1829, they established themselves among the foremost manufacturers of locomotives in the country.

After Robert Stephenson's death his cousin George Robert Stephenson became Managing Director of the firm and he in turn was succeeded by his two sons George and Robert. It has now been absorbed by the General Electric and English Electric Companies.

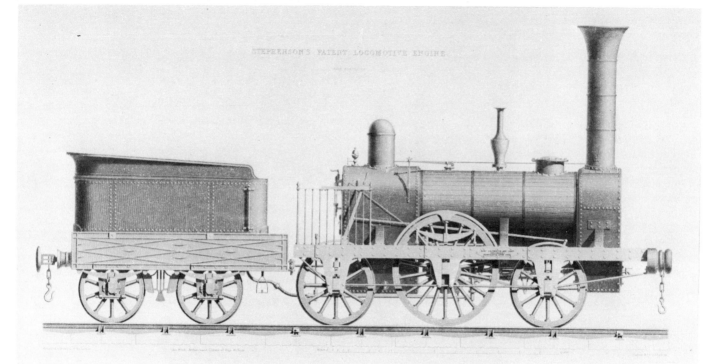

Garnkirk and Glasgow Railway
Opening

Lettered with title and From nature & on stone by D. O. Hill S.A.. W. Day, Lithr. to the King, 17, Gate St. London.
Lithograph, coloured by hand
$12\frac{3}{8}$ in × 18 in (31·3 cm × 45·6 cm)

The railway, which was nearly nine miles long, received Parliamentary approval in 1826 and was formally opened on 27 September 1831. It was mainly sponsored by the Tennant brothers, who owned a large chemical works adjoining the canal basin at Townhead in Glasgow, and who found that the canal could no longer provide coal in sufficient quantity to meet their demands. The construction of the railway presented many problems to Grainger and Miller, the engineers, because much of it passed over moss and peat bogs. From the outset it was in competition with the Monkland and Kirkintilloch Railway, which ran from Palacecraig, near Airdrie, to the Forth and Clyde canal and had been opened in 1826, and in order to win support and publicity for their enterprise the Directors of the Garnkirk and Glasgow staged an elaborate opening to which civic and other dignitaries were invited. Two locomotives had been ordered from the Stephensons and both operated on that day, one, the 'St. Rollox' driven by Robert Stephenson himself, taking passengers out to Coatbridge while the other came in from Monklands laden with coal and minerals.

The Garnkirk and Glasgow Railway was acquired by the Caledonian Railway in 1846.

Liverpool and Manchester Railway
View at Newton

Lettered with title and Drawn by Calvert. Aquatint by Havell *and dated* 1825.
Aquatint, coloured by hand
$9\frac{3}{4}$ in × 12 in (24·8 cm × 30·4 cm)

The vast increase in cotton manufacture in Manchester during the early nineteenth century and corresponding increase in the quantity of traffic to Liverpool, the nearest port, high-lighted the inadequacy of the Mersey and Irwell, and Bridgwater canals as a means of transportation between the cities. Consequently, when in 1824 a railway was suggested, it was warmly welcomed. An Act authorising the new line was passed on 5 May 1826 after construction work had already begun under the direction of George Stephenson, the engineer of the earlier Stockton and Darlington line, and the railway was formally opened on 15 September 1830. It was thirty-one miles long and cost a little under one million pounds. One event, in particular, marred the opening celebrations. William Huskisson, one of the Members of Parliament for Liverpool and one of the railway's staunchest supporters, was run over by a train at Parkside, near Newton, some seventeen miles from Liverpool, and later died. It was questioned whether the ceremony should continue but, when the size of the reception which had been arranged for the party at Liverpool was pointed out to the Duke of Wellington, who was one of the guests, he decided that they should continue, but that the festivities should be cut short.

The Liverpool and Manchester Railway was absorbed with the Bolton and Leigh, and Kenyon and Leigh Railways in 1845 to form the Grand Junction Railway, and in the following year the Grand Junction itself became part of the London and North Western Railway.

This print depicts an imaginary view, because construction of the railway had not begun at Newton at the time that it was drawn.

Liverpool and Manchester Railway
The tunnel

Lettered with title and T. T. Bury, delt.. H. Pyall sculpt.. London, published Feby. 1, 1831 by R. Ackermann, 96, Strand.
Aquatint, coloured by hand
$9\frac{3}{4}$ in × $12\frac{1}{8}$ in (25 cm × 30·7 cm)
Plate from T. T. Bury, *Coloured Views on the Liverpool and Manchester Railway*, 1834.

The tunnel constructed under Liverpool took eighteen months to build and was opened on 7 June 1828. During the summer of the following year sightseers were allowed to visit it and the tunnel immediately became a place of great interest to the inhabitants of the city and their friends. The roof was whitewashed and gas lights were suspended from it, initially at intervals of fifty yards, but later every twenty-five yards. The company charged one shilling per visit, which allowed the entire length to be inspected. On several occasions the harmonic band played while the sightseers strolled. Contemporary newspapers reported that large crowds visited the tunnel whenever it was open, and on the 21 August, when William Huskisson inspected it, an estimated three thousand paid to see the sights. Huskisson's enthusiasm, sadly curtailed by his death during the opening celebrations, was such that he encouraged others to visit not only the tunnel, but also the operations at Chat Moss and other major works on which the company were engaged.

Liverpool and Manchester Railway
Rainhill bridge

Lettered with title and T. T. Bury, delt.. H. Pyall, sculpt.. London, Pubd. by R. Ackermann, 96, Strand, 1831.
Aquatint, coloured by hand
$9\frac{7}{8}$ in × $11\frac{1}{4}$ in (25 cm × 28·5 cm)
Plate from T. T. Bury, *Coloured Views on the Liverpool and Manchester Railway*, 1834.

The skew bridge at Rainhill, ten miles east of Liverpool, carried the Liverpool and Warrington turnpike road over the railway and was completed in 1829. The main interest of the bridge is that it marks the point at which the famous Rainhill trials were held. The Directors of the Company had originally considered using stationary engines to work the new line, but Stephenson strongly opposed this, and they eventually agreed to test the merits of moving engines in a competition for which a prize of £500 was to be offered for the best locomotive that should fulfil certain stipulated conditions. The site at Rainhill was chosen because it was both straight and flat. On 6 October, the first day of the trials, four steam locomotives and one horse machine had assembled to compete for the prize. Although the 'Novelty' entered by Ericsson, a Swedish inventor, and John Braithwaite was the popular favourite, it broke down on the second of its timed runs, and the competition centred instead on the 'Sans Pareil' entered by Timothy Hackworth and the 'Rocket' entered by the Stephensons. These two engines put up similar times until on its eighth run the 'Sans Pareil' also broke down. The 'Rocket' alone performed perfectly and met all the required conditions, and was declared the winner. As has often been stressed, this was a crucial turning point in railway history because it confirmed beyond all measure of doubt the superiority of steam driven trains over those pulled by horses.

The 'Rocket', and the 'Sans Pareil' are now on display in the Science Museum.

Liverpool and Manchester Railway
Chat Moss

Lettered with title and Drawn & engraved by I. Shaw. Published March 13th, 1831 by I. Shaw, Post Office Place, Liverpool. *Engraving, coloured by hand*
$7\frac{3}{8}$ in × $9\frac{1}{2}$ in (18·7 cm × 24 cm)

After Stephenson had divided the Liverpool and Manchester Railway into three sections and appointed his pupils as resident engineers, John Dixon found himself faced with the problem of constructing the four mile crossing over Chat Moss, about which one eminent engineer had said 'no engineer in his senses would go through Chat Moss . . . a railroad certainly cannot be safely made over it without going to the bottom'. These remarks were brought home to Dixon, who, while surveying, slipped off one of the wooden planks laid across the bog and sank to his waist. Nobody appears to have known to what depth the bog extended, but Stephenson's intention was to float the railway over it on a mattress of heather and brushwood. Men were employed to cut these materials, which were then tipped with rubble into the bog; but load followed load, and even after several weeks still continued to sink beneath the surface. The Directors held a board meeting at the Moss to consider an alternative route but Stephenson persuaded them to persevere and eventually a solid embankment was built and opened by 1 January 1830. Opponents of the scheme had forecast that it would cost three quarters of a million pounds, but in the event it worked out at the comparatively reasonable sum of twenty-eight thousand pounds.

Dublin and Kingstown Railway
The tunnel from the excavation, looking towards Dublin

Lettered with title and A. Nichol, delt.. J. Harris, sculpt.. Dublin, published by W. F. Wakeman, 9 D'Olier Street, October 1834.
Aquatint, coloured by hand
9⅞ in × 11⅞ in (25 cm × 30 cm)
Plate from *Five Views of the Dublin and Kingstown Railway from drawings by Andrew Nichol*, 1834.

Although an Act was passed in May 1826 authorising the construction of a line between Waterford and Limerick, it was never carried out and consequently the Dublin and Kingstown Railway, which received authorisation on 6 September 1831, was the first Irish railway. The construction of the line, which covered a distance of six miles from Westland Row, Dublin, to Kingstown Bay and had intermediate stations at Booteestown, Blackrock and Salthill, was supervised by Charles Vignoles. Vignoles, a retired army officer had earlier been involved with the Liverpool and Manchester Railway. At one time the Dublin and Kingstown was operated using the atmospheric system but that was abandoned in 1856.

Before 1841 the company used locomotives built by G. Forrester of Liverpool but later they set up their own locomotive works at Dublin. A model of one of these later locomotives, named the 'Alexandra' after it had hauled the train used by the Prince and Princess of Wales on their official visit to Dublin in 1865, is now in the Science Museum.

The Dublin and Kingstown remained a separate company until 1925, when in the regrouping of the Irish railways it was absorbed by the Great Southern.

Bodmin and Wadebridge Railway
Opening

Lettered with title and Which was constructed under the directions of Messrs. Roger Hopkins and Sons, Civil Engineers, and was publicly opened on the 30th of September, 1834; on which occasion the Camel engine drew 22 carriages containing more than 400 persons. This view shows the train in the act of passing over Pendevy Bridge. C. Ingrey lithog. 310 Strand, London.
Lithograph, coloured by hand
$11\frac{3}{8}$ in $\times$ $34\frac{1}{4}$ in (29 cm $\times$ 86·9 cm)

The Bodmin and Wadebridge Railway, which was sanctioned in 1832 and opened throughout two years later, was Cornwall's first locomotive line. Covering a distance of twenty miles, it ran from Wadebridge to Wenford Bridge. Constructed primarily to transport sea-sand for manure and minerals for export, the complete line with two engines and forty wagons cost the surprisingly small sum of thirty-five thousand pounds, most of which was borne by local inhabitants.

The Bodmin and Wadebridge was sold to the Devon and Cornwall Central Railway in 1845 and then to the London and South Western in 1847. It was not however legally absorbed until 1886 and not linked with the London and South Western until 1895.

Two of the first coaches from the railway dating from the 1830s, now in the railway museum at York, are thought to be the earliest surviving passenger coaches in the country.

London and Greenwich Railway

Lettered with title and an account of the formation and objectives of the London and Greenwich Railway Company.
Lithograph, coloured by hand
$12\frac{5}{8}$ in × $17\frac{3}{8}$ in (32·3 cm × 44·1 cm)

The London and Greenwich was not only London's first railway but was also the only railway to be built entirely on a single viaduct. George Walter projected the line in 1831 and acted as the secretary of a company formed to build it, but the suggestion that it should be built on a viaduct was made by Lt.-Col Landmann, who also provided the designs. Landmann laid the first brick, in open country near Corbett's Lane, on 4 April 1834, and supervised the work of construction, which was undertaken by Hugh McIntosh. After much difficulty in purchasing the necessary land, which involved negotiations with some five hundred separate parties, and in constructing a drawbridge over the navigable River Ravensbourne, the whole line was opened in the winter of 1838, although the stations at Greenwich and London Bridge were not completed until several years later. Some of the arches were fitted up as houses, but it was found that rain water leaked in through holes in the brickwork caused by the constant vibration of the stone blocks carrying the rails. These were replaced with wooden sleepers but the arches still failed to attract permanent residents and were sold instead for storage purposes.

One peculiarity of the railway was that the down track was on the right and the up track on the left, but this was changed in 1901, when the usual plan was introduced. The viaduct is still in everyday use although it has now been widened to accommodate twelve sets of rails.

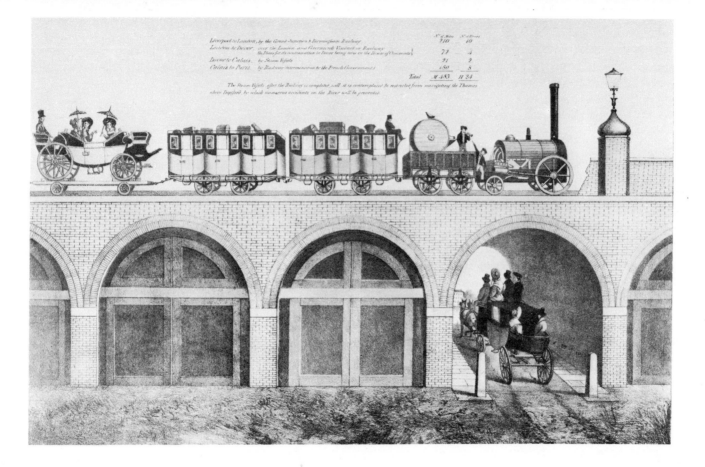

London and Birmingham Railway
Entrance portico, Euston Grove station

Lettered with title and **J. C. Bourne del. et lith.. London, published Septr. 1 1838 by J. C. Bourne 19, Lamb's Conduit St. & Ackermann & Co. Strand. Printed by Day & Haghe Lithrs. to the Queen.**
Lithograph, coloured by hand
10⅛ in × 15⅝ in (25·7 cm × 39·6 cm)
Plate from **J. C. Bourne,** *Drawings of the London and Birmingham Railway,* 1839.

The famous Euston Arch, designed by Philip Hardwick in 1836 and so sadly demolished in 1962, symbolised the pride felt by the Directors of the London and Birmingham Railway Company in their enormous achievement. The Company had been formed as early as 1823 but the necessary parliamentary approval for the undertaking was not received until 6 May 1833. There were several reasons for this delay. The members of the Company were divided as to whether the line should pass through Oxford or Coventry, a question which was not resolved until 1830 when George Stephenson, the Company's engineer, selected the Coventry route. Difficulties had also arisen, over the choice of site for the London terminus, and through the failure in the House of Lords of the first Bill presented to Parliament.

The first sod was cut at Chalk Farm on 1 June 1834, and the first section of the line, from Euston to Boxmoor, a distance of twenty-four and a half miles, opened for passengers and goods three years later. The whole line was opened on 17 September 1838, when it was reputed to have cost five and a half million pounds. That the entire work should have been completed in a little over four years was mainly due to Stephenson's administrative ability in supervising twenty-nine separate contracts—no firms at that time were considered to be large enough to undertake more than six miles of line—and in his ability to spend long hours travelling along the works, inspecting progress and dealing with problems as they arose.

London and Birmingham Railway
The station at Euston Square

Lettered with title and T. T. Bury, delt.. J. Harris sculpt.. London, published September 18th 1837 by Ackermann & Co. 96 Strand.
Aquatint, coloured by hand
9¼ in × 10⅝ in (23·5 cm × 26·9 cm)
Plate from T. T. Bury, *Six Views of the London and Birmingham Railway*, 1837.

The station at Euston behind Hardwick's colossal propylaeum was let to the Cubitt brothers, as contractors, in December 1835. Unlike the rest of the line, the approach involved the construction of a steep gradient and other problems; the Regent's Canal had to be crossed and many bridges provided for future roads. The four lines of track—it was originally anticipated that the Great Western Railway would also use the terminus—ran in a cutting through high retaining walls which were difficult to build because of the treacherous nature of the blue lias clay they supported. The shed itself covered an area of ten thousand square feet and contained parts of offices besides the arrival and departure platforms. Carriages were turned on turntables inside the station rather than in sidings because of the shortage of space.

The steep gradient leading out of the station meant that locomotives did not originally come into Euston. Porters pushed the carriages out of the shed to a point near the bridge under Wriothesley Street where they were attached to a large rope which hauled them at a speed approaching twenty miles an hour to the depot at Camden Town where the locomotives waited. Bourne records that this continuous rope 'passes round large wheels at the extremities of the plane, and over a number of small sleeves, or pulleys, fixed along the centre of the track-way, it is 3,744 yards long and seven inches in circumference'.

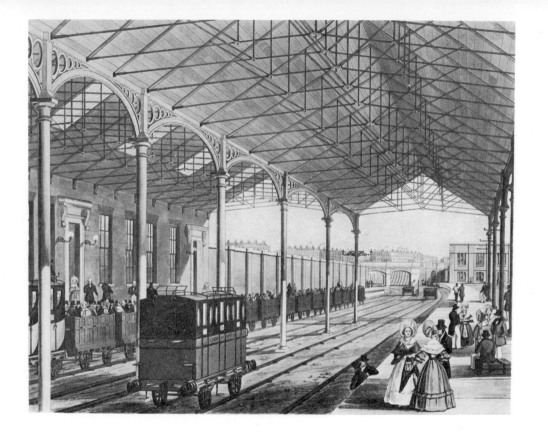

London and Birmingham Railway
Camden Town depot

Lettered J. C. Bourne del. et lith.. Eccentric for shifting rail. Locomotive engine-house. Chimnies of stationary engine-house. Published July 1838 by the Proprietor J. C. Bourne 19, Lambs Conduit Street, and Ackermann & Co. Strand, London. Day and Haghe Lithrs. to the Queen, *and stamped in blind* Specimen Bourne's [Drawings] of the London and Birmingham Railway.
Lithograph, coloured by hand
$10\frac{3}{8}$ in × $13\frac{1}{4}$ in (26·2 cm × 33·5 cm)
Plate from J. C. Bourne, *Drawings of the London and Birmingham Railway*, 1839.

It had originally been intended that the London terminus of the railway should be formed at Camden Town, and, even after the station at Euston had been built, Camden continued to be used for cattle and heavy goods. Bourne recorded that 'this Dépôt covers a space of more than thirty acres, and comprises, amongst other buildings, a locomotive engine-house of considerable extent. In the latter the engines are stored, as they arrive with trains; it contains an office for registering the arrival and departure of each; workshops for repairing them; with lathes, furnaces, anvils, and other necessary conveniences, both for the light and heavy work connected with repairs; and tanks in the roof, filled from a deep well by means of a steam engine, and used to supply the engines with water on their departure. The building is entirely fire-proof, and occupies three-quarters of an acre. The Camden Town Dépôt includes also, spacious and convenient offices for the Goods Department; warehouses and store-rooms; repositories, or stables, for cattle; and sheds for protecting the wagons; besides a dépôt for a large supply of coal, and a number of ovens for converting it into coke for the use of the engines'. The tall chimneys on the right carried away smoke from the stationary engines used to haul the trains up from Euston.

The Roundhouse Theatre at Camden Town occupies one of the original buildings used by the railway.

London and Birmingham Railway
Kilsby Tunnel

Two views on one sheet lettered Working-shaft, July 8th 1837 *and* Great ventilating shaft. J. C. Bourne del. et lith..
Printed by Day & Haghe lithrs. to the Queen. London, published Decr. 1838 by the proprietor J. C. Bourne 19, Lambs
Conduit St. & Ackermann & Co. Strand.
Lithograph, coloured by hand
9½ in × 15⅝ in (24·7 cm × 39·8 cm)
Plates from J. C. Bourne, *Drawings of the London and Birmingham Railway*, 1839.

All other problems which arose during the construction of the London and Birmingham Railway paled beside those encountered while building the tunnel at Kilsby. It had originally been intended to route the line through Northampton, but that scheme was abandoned because of the opposition of local landowners, and George Stephenson, the Company's engineer, was reported to prefer a tunnel to the west rather than be faced with the difficult task of crossing the Nene valley. Later when the Roade to Rugby link was built, which connected Northampton to the main line, it was found that a tunnel was necessary anyway.

The main problem at Kilsby was not just that a railway tunnel as long as 2,400 yards had not previously been built, but that subterranean quicksands, not detected during the surveys, continually drowned out the workings. Stephenson, who had been warned of the dangers by Dr Arnold, who owned property at Kilsby, had originally planned to sink eight working shafts and two ventilating shafts, but in spite of cutting driftways to the sides of the tunnel with the object of drawing off sand and water, it eventually became necessary to more than double the number of working shafts. These were arranged in pairs and joined under the ground so that water could be kept from one by pumping it out of the other. Only after thirteen pumps had moved nearly two thousand gallons of water a minute for nine months did the shafts become workable. By this time the tunnel was so far behind schedule that it became necessary to employ teams of navvies labouring continuously day and night in shifts before it was completed, four years after the work had first begun. The presence of so many workmen in the quiet village of Kilsby so upset the local inhabitants that troops had to be called in to keep the peace.

Birmingham and Gloucester Railway
Defford Bridge on the River Avon

Lettered with title and Span of each arch, 58 feet—height above water line, 28 feet. Captn. W. S. Moorsom, Engr. E. I. Dolby, del.. Clerk & Co. lithog. 202, High Holborn. Published by R. A. Sprigg, Architectural Library, 109 Gt. Russell St. Bedford Sqr.. *Dated* 1839.
Lithograph, coloured by hand
11⅝ in × 16¼ in (29·5 cm × 40·3 cm)

On 22 April 1836 a Bill was passed authorising the construction of a line from Camp Hill, Birmingham, to Gloucester, a distance of fifty miles. The line was primarily intended to avoid the long journey through London which would be necessary when the Great Western's line was opened, but also to provide Birmingham with a direct means of access to the West Country ports. Moorsom, the Company's engineer, surveyed three routes and eventually chose that through Moseley, Bromsgrove, Dunhampstead, Spetchley, Ashchurch and Cheltenham, terminating at the Gloucestershire and Berkeley's Canal Company's basin and docks at Gloucester. One important clause in the original Bill allowed the company to form a junction with the London and Birmingham Railway, something which the latter had encouraged because it helped to confine the broad gauge to the south, and on 17 August 1841, after the remainder of the railway had been completed, the extension from Camp Hill to the Curzon Street station at Birmingham was opened.

Perhaps the most famous feature of the Birmingham and Gloucester was the two mile Lickey Incline between Blackwell and Bromsgrove with a gradient of 1 in 37. This was so steep that Moorsom was obliged to purchase locomotives which he had seen ascending similar inclines in America, from Norris, a locomotive builder of Philadelphia. The chief peculiarity of these engines was that they had much smaller driving wheels than those used in this country and also a swivelling front bogie, and until J. E. McConell built at the Company's Bromsgrove works a special tank locomotive, the American engines were not superseded.

The Birmingham and Gloucester, the first railway to use printed tickets, amalgamated with the Bristol and Gloucester in 1845 to form the Bristol and Birmingham, but in the following year these two small companies were dissolved and their property was invested in the Midland Railway.

Newcastle, North Shields and Tynemouth Railway
The Ouse Burn Viaduct

Lettered with title, details of the construction, and John and Benjamin Green, Architects and Engineers 1838. T. M. Richardson Senr. del & lithogr. A. Ducôté's lithogy. 70 St. Martins Lane, London. Published by T. McLean, 26, Haymarket & F. Loraine, Grey St., Newcastle upon Tyne.
Lithograph, coloured by hand
$12\frac{3}{4}$ in × 17 in (32·5 cm × 43·2 cm)

The proposal to build a line from Newcastle to North Shields as part of what would eventually form the east coast route to Scotland was first made in 1830. There were two different schools of thought as to which route the new line should follow, and it was not until an independent arbitrator had been consulted that the route from Shield Field, Newcastle, through Old Walker and Wallsend to Saville Street, North Shields, was selected. Parliament passed the Bill on 21 June 1836, at which time it was agreed that the proposed branch line to Tynemouth should in fact form part of the main line.

The construction involved two viaducts of particular interest, across the Ouseburn and Willington Dene valleys. The latter was the longer of the two, with seven main arches, but it was only eight-two feet above ground, whereas the shorter Ouseburn was one hundred and eight feet high. Both were constructed entirely of laminated timber arches resting on masonry piers, similar to the Wiebeking system used to build the Pont d'Ivry across the River Seine in Paris. The viaducts and railway were opened on 18 June 1839 during one of the most violent thunderstorms in living memory, but the Tynemouth extension was not ready for traffic until 29 March 1847.

London and Brighton Railway, Shoreham branch
Opening

Lettered This print in commemoration of the opening of the Shoreham branch of the London & Brighton Railway, is respectfully dedicated to the shareholders, by their obedient servant, W. H. Mason. Drawn by H. G. Hine. Published by W. H. Mason at his Repository of Arts, Rrighton [sic]. Printed by Lefevre, Newman St.
Lithograph, coloured by hand
$9\frac{1}{2}$ in × $12\frac{1}{8}$ in (24 cm × 30·8 cm)

On 15 July 1837 an Act of Parliament was passed authorising the London and Brighton Railway Company to build a line from a junction with the London and Croydon Railway at Norwood to Brighton and to form branches to Shoreham, Lewes and Newhaven. The branch along the coast from Brighton to Shoreham was the first part of the railway to be completed, and opened on 12 May 1840. At that time it was hoped that a steamer service would be operated between Shoreham and Dieppe, but the plan fell through and vessels left instead from Newhaven. The complete line from Norwood to Brighton was opened on 1 September 1841.

One of the Directors of the London and Brighton, Rowland Hill, the Post Office reformer, was responsible for introducing excursion trains, the first running on Easter Monday 1844. It consisted of forty-five carriages drawn by four engines, but at New Cross six more carriages and another engine were attached, and a sixth engine and another six carriages at Croydon. The party reached Brighton at 1-30 p.m., four and a half hours after setting out.

Although the Company had powers to build the branches to Lewes and Newhaven too, only the last was carried out at the time, the other being built later by a different company. In 1846 the line from Shoreham was extended to Chichester, and in 1923 it became part of the Southern Railway.

Great North of England Railway
Oblique bridge over the River Tees near Croft

Lettered with title and Angle of obliquity 50°—span of each arch on the oblique face 60 feet. Designed and executed by Henry Welch, Civil Engineer, 1840. G. Hawkins lith. Painted by J. H. Richardson. Day & Haghe, Lithrs. to the Queen. Published by Currie and Garthwaite, Newcastle upon Tyne.
Lithograph, coloured by hand
14⅝ in × 19⅞ in (37·2 cm × 50·5 cm)

Realising that few of the early railway lines in the north of England ran from north to south rather than from east to west, the Directors of the Stockton and Darlington Railway projected a Great North of England Railway in 1835 and in the following year the consent of Parliament was obtained for a line between Newcastle and York. The project involved few complex engineering works, the most notable being the Eryholme cutting between Croft and Dalton, the embankment past Northallerton, and the bridges over the Tees near Croft and the Ouse at Nether Poppleton near York. The bridge over the Tees, designed by Henry Welch, with a length of four hundred and seventy-one feet was, at the time of construction, one of the largest skew bridges in the country. Other bridges over the line, designed by Thomas Storey, were not so successful and collapsed soon after erection, and he was obliged to resign. In spite of so few engineering works, Robert Stephenson, Storey's successor as the Company's engineer, was able to report to the Directors at the time of the opening in 1841, that the railway had been laid on 'straight lines to an extent unparalleled in this country'.

In 1846 the Great North of England was absorbed by the Newcastle and Darlington Railway when the title the York and Newcastle Railway was adopted and after further amalgamations this became part of the North Eastern Railway.

Great Western Railway
Kelston Bridge near Bath

Lettered with title and On stone by L. Haghe, Esqre.. Printed by Lavars & Ackland, Bristol. London: Hamilton, Adams & Co.. Bristol: Lavars & Ackland.
Lithograph, coloured by hand
8¾ in × 11 in (21·2 cm × 27·9 cm)
Plate from [W. W. Young and] L. Haghe, *Illustrations of the Great Western and Bristol and Exeter Railways*, 1840.

During the mid 1820s many schemes were put forward for lines between Bristol and London, the most interesting of which was that proposed by John Loudon McAdam for a London to Bristol Rail Road Company, but all fell through because of lack of support. In 1832 McAdam's scheme was revived and Isambard Kingdom Brunel appointed to survey a route. Parliamentary approval for the line was received on 31 August 1835, by which time it had become known as the Great Western Railway. Several other companies also began building lines from Bristol at this date but the Great Western was the first to open, a train running from Bristol to Bath on 31 August 1840, and the first train to London on 30 June 1841. By 1844, however, Bristol could boast of connections with Exeter and Birmingham also.

One early decision of the Great Western was to build the new railway using a seven foot gauge rather than the more usual four feet eight and a half inches, because Brunel believed that more powerful locomotives could then be used and higher speeds achieved. The wider gauge also allowed the construction of more comfortable coaches. This decision was to prove very costly and to have far-reaching effects, for the findings of the gauge commission, which sat in 1845, in favour of the narrower width, and the greater quantity of that gauge which had already been constructed particularly in the north, meant that all the broad gauge had eventually to be replaced. In the mean-time, complicated arrangements involving the transfer of goods and passengers, or the construction of three lines of track, were requisite wherever the different gauges met.

Great Western Railway
Bridge over the Uxbridge Road near Hanwell

Lettered with title and From nature & on stone by **J. C. Bourne**. Printed by **C. F. Cheffins**.
Lithograph, coloured by hand
12¼ in × 16⅛ in (31·1 cm × 40·9 cm)
Plate from J. C. Bourne, *History and Description of the Great Western Railway*, 1846.

At the point where the Great Western Railway crossed the junction of the Uxbridge Road and the road between Brentford and Greenford, to the west of the Wharncliffe viaduct, Brunel designed a skew bridge which was remarkable not simply for its strange design—at first glance it could almost be mistaken for a modern motorway bridge—but for the trouble it caused. The construction involved cast iron and brick columns supporting cast iron girders. In March 1839 one of the main girders collapsed and as a result of the repair all the brick infilling, on which the track partly rested, was replaced with timber. Eight years later a red hot coal from a passing train caused this to catch fire and the heat was so intense that nearly every girder in the bridge was broken. After being shored up, the cast iron was replaced with wrought iron, and Brunel later wrote 'cast iron girder bridges are always giving trouble, our Great Western road bridge at Hanwell which since 1838 has always been under repair . . . has cost its first cost three times over . . . I never use cast iron if I can help it'.

Underneath the left hand side of the bridge, in the distance, can be seen the buildings of the Middlesex County Lunatic Asylum.

Great Western Railway
West front of No. 1 tunnel

Lithograph, coloured by hand
Cut to 12$\frac{7}{8}$ in × 11$\frac{1}{2}$ in (32·8 cm × 29·2 cm)
Frontispiece to J. Bourne, *History and Description of the Great Western Railway*, 1846.

The works between Bristol and Bath were some of the heaviest on the line, involving two stations and a series of cuttings, tunnels, viaducts and bridges. The three tunnels outside Bristol, Nos. 1, 2 and 3, were contracted out to William Ranger, but Brunel had great trouble with him because he lacked sufficient capital and energy, and in 1838 he was removed and the work was continued by the company's engineers. No. 1 tunnel was completed by August 1839. In 1887 it was opened out during the construction of new marshalling yards at Bristol East Depot.

Brunel had ordered the original locomotives used on the Great Western from various manufacturers, and since he left the design to them, started with a strange assortment, none of which worked particularly well. In 1837, however, Daniel Gooch offered his services as a locomotive builder and was promptly hired by Brunel to manage the locomotive workshops. Gooch, and another young engineer, T. R. Crampton, produced their first locomotive, the 'Firefly', in 1840 and it was immediately far more successful than its predecessors. On its first run the locomotive travelled at the astonishing speed of fifty-eight miles an hour. The 'Acheron' depicted here was one of sixty-two later locomotives which were built to the same design. The most famous of the 'Firefly' class was probably the 'Actaeon', which on 1 May 1844, with Gooch himself as driver, travelled three hundred and eighty-seven miles to Exeter and back, in one day, at an average speed of almost forty miles an hour, certainly the most spectacular locomotive performance the world had witnessed to that time.

Great Western Railway
Engine house, Swindon

Lettered with title and Sketched & drawn on stone by J. C. Bourne. Printed by C. F. Cheffins.
Lithograph, coloured by hand
12⅜ in × 16⅛ in (31·3 cm × 40·9 cm)
Plate from J. C. Bourne, *History and Description of the Great Western Railway*, 1846.

Swindon was selected in 1840 as the site for the Great Western Railway's principal depot and repair workshops, partly because it was situated conveniently between London and Bristol and was at the junction of the Cheltenham Railway, but also because it was close to the Wiltshire and Berkshire canal along which supplies of coal could be brought. The repair workshops were situated to the west of the passenger station on the north side of the line, and were described by Bourne as follows: 'In the centre of and at right angles to this shed [the engine storage shed], and abutting against its northern side, is the Engine house; this is an oblong room, 290 feet by 140, and divided by two rows of columns into three compartments; the engines stand in the side compartments, transversely, as horses in the stalls of a stable; and the central part, 50 feet broad, is occupied by a large platform, travelling on wheels from one end of the house to the other, and by means of which an engine can be readily transferred between the central part and any one of the stalls. Here the engines receive their lighter repairs, those which the enginemen themselves are for the most part capable of executing. The roof of this shed is of timber and wrought iron, covered in with slating; and the stalls will contain thirty-six engines and tenders'.

After the publication of Bourne's description the size of the engine works at Swindon rapidly increased, and by 1849, when economies caused a cut back in the labour force, 1,800 men were being employed and the works covered more than fourteen acres. Much still survives including the rows of houses, laid out, apparently by Sir Matthew Digby Wyatt, for the railway employees, and there is now a Great Western Railway museum there too.

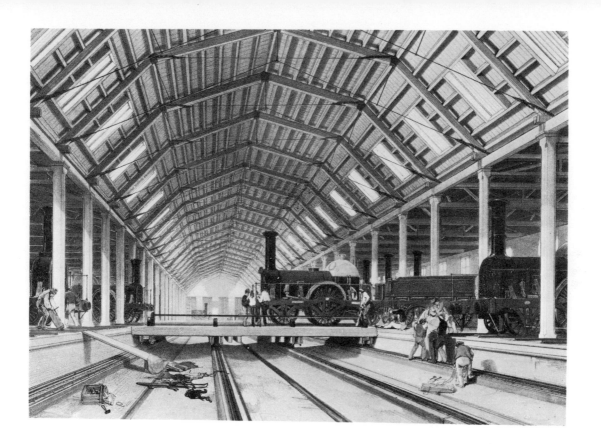

South Eastern Railway
Shakespeare tunnel and viaduct

Lettered with title and W. Cubitt F.R.S. etc. engineer. Lithographed by Clerk & Co. 202 High Holborn, where railway plans, sections, and every other description of plans & drawings are executed.
Lithograph, coloured by hand
12 in × 15⅝ in (30·5 cm × 39·1 cm)

The Shakespeare tunnel and viaduct formed part of the six miles of line between Dover and Folkestone which was opened on 7 February 1844. The construction of this comparatively short distance involved a series of very considerable engineering works. After leaving Folkestone the railway crossed the valley between Charlton Down and East Wear Bay by a viaduct of nineteen arches. This was succeeded by the Tower tunnel, one third of a mile in length, Warren's cutting, two miles long, the Abbot's Cliff tunnel, over one mile long, a further cutting and wall at sea level, and finally the Shakespeare tunnel and viaduct.

In order to overcome the problem of building a fourth tunnel at the approach to the Shakespeare cliff, a large part of the Round Down Cliff estimated at more than a million tons of chalk, was removed by a single blast of 185 barrels of gunpowder, on 26 January 1843. William Cubitt (later Sir William Cubitt), the engineer of these works, could not be as sure of the structural solidity of the Shakespeare Cliff as he had been of the Abbot's Cliff, and decided to build the tunnel through it with a central pier, and to line most of the inside with brick. It was ventilated by seven shafts passing to the top of the cliff and eight galleries running to the sea, the latter also served as passages for the removal of rubble during the building operations.

The tunnel still survives but the viaduct was removed in 1927, when extensions involved building more than two lines of track.

South Devon Railway
Viaduct over the valley of the Erme at Ivy Bridge

Signed W. Dawson *and dated* 29 Augt. 1848. *Lettered with title and* On stone and printed by W. Spreat, Exeter.
Colour lithograph
12½ in × 20⅛ in (30·8 cm × 51·1 cm)

The first prospects for a railway in South Devon appeared in 1843 under the title of the Plymouth, Devonport and Exeter Railway, but by 4 July 1844, when the Act authorising a broad gauge railway in continuation of the Bristol and Exeter was passed, it became known as the South Devon. The Railway is perhaps best known for the abortive attempts which were made by Brunel, the company's engineer, to introduce the so-called atmospheric system of working between 1847 and 1848. The system worked through the action of a piston, attached to the train, in an airtight tube running between the rails. As air was evacuated from the tube by pumps along the line, so the piston and thus the train, were drawn along. In theory such a method of working was sound and had the advantage of being comparatively cheap to run, but in practice many complications arose, not the least of which was that the rails could not easily cross, and that the continuous leather valve in the top of the tube constantly broke down.

Architecturally the line was distinguished for the timber viaducts which Brunel designed at Bittaford, Blachford, Glaze, Slade and Ivybridge. All were more than two hundred yards long and over one hundred feet high, and consisted of frail-looking tapering masonry piers supporting timber framing. They were originally designed for the single track atmospheric railway, and when steam was introduced apparently vibrated alarmingly. They were strengthened in the early 1860s by iron girders added under the flooring, but when the line was doubled in 1893, were demolished and replaced with new structures. Similarly the timber viaducts which Brunel designed in Cornwall have all now disappeared.

The South Devon initially used its own rolling stock and staff but hired locomotives from the Great Western Railway, and in 1878 the two companies were amalgamated.

South Devon Railway
Landslip near the Parson and Clerk Rock between Dawlish and Teignmouth December 29th 1852

Lettered with title and On stone by F. Jones, W. Spreat, lithographer, Exeter. Published by L. Westcott, Dawlish.
Lithograph, coloured by hand
13⅞ in × 17½ in (35·3 cm × 44·3 cm)

'The late gales, and the long-continued wet weather, have had a serious effect upon the South Devon Railway' reported the *Illustrated London News* early in 1853. 'During last week, the traffic was partially interrupted by an immense slip or fall of the cliff . . . before the rails could be cleared the passengers and luggage were conveyed over the turnpike road, from Dawlish to Teigmouth, about four miles. All the vehicles and horses that could be procured in these towns were put into requisition for this service; and there was for a day or two a revival of the old-fashioned modes of travelling, to the great satisfaction of the turnpike-gate keepers . . . As soon as a portion of the mass lying on the rails had been cleared the trains resumed running up to the slip, and then discharged their passengers and luggage. The passengers walked across the damaged portion, and entered a train waiting on the other side. This arrangement necessarily caused a considerable delay in the arrival of trains; otherwise, no serious inconvenience resulted. A large number of labourers were employed day and night, in clearing the rubbish; and the damaged sea-wall will have to be rebuilt. The scene at night, with the large fires of the workmen, the roaring of the sea immediately below the line, and other accessories, was very striking'.

Similar problems had arisen during the construction of the difficult sea-wall. Gales caused damage before the mortar had set, and the action of the sand on the beach, because there were no groins, caused erosion of the foundations. There were further disasters in February 1855 when fifty feet of the wall were washed away, and in 1873, but it has suffered comparatively little damage since.

Manchester and Leeds Railway
Victoria station, Hunt's Bank, Manchester

Lettered with title and A. F. Tait, del. & lith.. Day & Haghe Lithrs. to the Queen.
Lithograph, coloured by hand
$10\frac{1}{4}$ in × $13\frac{5}{8}$ in (26·1 cm × 34·5 cm)
Plate from A. F. Tait and E. Butterworth, *Views on the Manchester and Leeds Railway*, 1845.

In April 1842 the Manchester and Leeds Railway agreed with the Liverpool and Manchester Railway that they should form extension lines to meet at Hunt's Bank, Manchester, where a joint station would be built. The former company had previously used a station at Oldham Road, Manchester, but passengers were transferred to the new station when it was completed in 1844. Later, a third company, the Manchester, Bolton and Preston Railway, also used the station and in consequence Manchester, Liverpool, Leeds and Hull all became accessible from it.

The shed, which was designed by George Stephenson and covered an area of eighty thousand square feet, was the largest in England of its date. Tait wrote that 'the appearance of the interior of this singularly splendid and vast cavernous-like avenue, when viewed from almost any point, is strikingly impressive; the ingeniously complicated forms of the ironwork of the roof, the range of skylights admitting glimpses of light from above, the colonnades of graceful pillars on each hand, the numerous trains of passenger carriages and goods waggons almost constantly in motion, either arriving or departing, the hustling movements of the railway officials and servants, the ever-changing groups of travellers passing to and from; the aged, the young, the opulent, and the humble . . . form altogether a most extraordinary scene, productive of ample material for useful and refined thought to a reflective mind'.

York and North Midland Railway
Crimple Valley viaduct

Lettered with title, details of the construction, and J. G. Birkinshaw Esqe. C. E.. Paviell and Sykes contractors. Gibson & Co. lith. artists & printers, York, Augt. 1847.
Lithograph, coloured by hand
10⅛ in × 12¾ in (26 cm × 32·5 cm)

The York and North Midland Railway Company received authorisation to construct a branch line from Church Fenton to Harrogate, via Tadcaster and Wetherby, in 1845. The line was opened as far as Spofforth on 10 August 1847, at which time it was reported that 'the Crimple Viaduct will, when completed, form one of the most wonderful of the achievements of science in railway construction in the kingdom. Its massy towering piers are now all reared, and its lofty expansive arches, stretching their wide concavities across the deep glen, will shortly be brought to a close'. The viaduct, and the Prospect Hill tunnel, 825 yards long, which led up to it, were in fact completed by 20 July 1848, when the new line was extended to the small Brunswick station at Harrogate.

The viaduct, designed by John Birkinshaw, remains one of the most impressive in the country. About one mile to the south east of Harrogate it consists of thirty-one arches of fifty feet span, the tallest of which is one hundred and twenty feet high. The Leeds and Thirsk line, later the Leeds Northern, which ran under the viaduct, did not have access to Harrogate, because of the range of hills known as the Almscliffe Bank, but in 1862 when improvements were made to the railway which included building a more central station at Harrogate, a connection between the lines was made and thenceforth trains from Leeds were enabled to reach Harrogate via Arthington.

Huddersfield and Sheffield Junction Railway
Lockwood viaduct

Lettered with title, details of the construction, and John Hawkshaw Esqr., Engineer, Messrs Miller, Blackie & Shortridge, contractors. Drawn and on stone by Alexr. Scott, Manchester. Maclure, Macdonald & Macgregor, Lithrs. Liverpool, London & Glasgow.
Lithograph, coloured by hand
17 in × 23⅝ in (43·1 cm × 60·3 cm)

The thirteen miles of line from Huddersfield to Penistone, where the Huddersfield and Sheffield joined the Manchester, Liverpool and Sheffield Railway, involved six tunnels and four major viaducts in addition to several deep cuttings, high embankments, and thirty bridges. The spectacular Lockwood viaduct, which was built using sandstone mined during making the cuttings and embankments by the Lockwood station and tunnel, was one of the largest structures of its kind in the country. Construction had begun in 1846 but was interrupted for long periods by labour problems and financial difficulties. The first arch was erected by August 1847 and the whole viaduct eventually completed in 1849. It was four hundred and seventy-six yards long and one hundred and thirty-six feet high and consisted of thirty-two semi-circular arches with two oblique arches over roads on either side of the valley. The cost was thirty-three thousand pounds.

Several attempts to close the line, which later became part of the Lancashire and Yorkshire Railway, have been made since 1960 but resisted by the Ministry of Transport, and the line still carries the regular passenger train service between Sheffield and Huddersfield.

Chester and Holyhead Railway
Britannia Bridge

Lettered with title and Anglesey entrance.
Engraving, coloured by hand
$12\frac{1}{2}$ in × 16 in (32 cm × 40·6 cm)

The line between Chester and Holyhead was originally projected by Robert Stephenson, who in 1836 had attempted to persuade the Directors of the Chester and Crewe Railway to extend their line to Holyhead. They rejected the proposal, however, as did the Directors of several other companies, on the grounds that the undertaking was too vast. Undeterred, Stephenson formed a new company, and obtained Parliamentary sanction for the line on 4 July 1844, although his proposal to bridge the Menai Straits was at first rejected and required further legislation before authorisation was received in the following year.

Three different sites for the Menai bridge were reviewed and that at the Britannia Rock eventually chosen. Stephenson's first design, for a bridge of two arches, was rejected by the Admiralty on the grounds that it would seriously impair navigation of the Straits, at which time he remarked 'I stood therefore on the verge of a responsibility from which I confess I had nearly shrunk, the construction of a tubular bridge of such gigantic dimensions did at first present itself as a difficulty of a very formidable nature'. Stephenson, however, persevered, and after many experiments, including one with circular tubes suspended by cables, evolved his final design. The first rivet was inserted on 10 August 1847, and by 20 June 1849 the first tube was floated successfully into position, at which time Stephenson, Brunel and other engineers toasted their success in champagne sitting on top of it. The earlier floating of the similar tubes designed by Stephenson for the bridge at Conway provided useful experience. After many mishaps and several fatalities the first train eventually passed over the bridge on 5 March 1850. The lions were carved by John Thomas, and the architecture, which, since it was begun before the decision to dispense with the suspension cables contained provision for them, was designed by Francis Thompson.

The bridge recently suffered heavy damage through fire, but has been repaired and continues in use.

BRITANNIA BRIDGE.
THE LARGE ENTRANCE.

Reading, Guildford and Reigate Railway
Bridge over the London and Bath Road, near Reading

Lettered with title and John Gardner Esqr. engineer. (Span 56 feet). Maclure, Macdonald & Macgregor, lithrs., London.
Lithograph, coloured by hand
12¼ in × 16 in (31·2 cm × 40·5 cm)

The Reading, Guildford and Reigate Railway was incorporated by an Act of Parliament in 1846 to build a line from Ash Junction near Aldershot, through Guildford to Shalford Junction. The railway left Reading on the Great Western line, crossed Berkshire by Wokingham and Sandhurst, entered Surrey by Frimley, ran along the base of the Hog's Back to Guildford and continued at the foot of the chalk hills past Dorking to Reigate and Redhill. The whole line was opened in July 1849 and gave Londoners their first access by rail to the large area of attractive countryside which included Box Hill.

The bridge was made using a system patented by John Gardner, an engineer of Wokingham, on 9 December 1848, and consisted of cast iron girders strengthened with wrought iron reinforcing bars. The locomotive about to cross it is one of Wilson's famous 'Jenny Lind' class, which, although comparatively small, were very lively and able to compete with larger locomotives because of their clever design and the fact that they worked at comparatively high steam pressures.

The Reading, Guildford and Reigate Railway was purchased in 1852 by the South Eastern Railway.

Central Railway Station, Newcastle-upon-Tyne

Lettered with title.
Lithograph, coloured by hand
Cut to 6 in × 9⅜ in (15·3 cm × 23·9 cm)

Since its opening on the 21 May 1839 the Newcastle and Carlisle Railway had used a temporary terminus at Newcastle near the shot tower, but in 1845 an agreement was made with the Newcastle and Berwick Railway to build a joint station, and John Dobson, a local architect, was commissioned to provide designs. He produced drawings showing an enormous 594 foot long frontage of classical columns but this scheme was subsequently modified, mainly for reasons of economy, although the huge porte cochère was retained. Behind this facade the shed was constructed in a graceful curve with three arched roofs, each of 60 foot span, supported on iron columns. The station was officially opened by Queen Victoria on 29 August 1850, the same day that she opened Robert Stephenson's famous Royal Border bridge at Berwick. A few days previously the station had been the venue for a large public dinner to George Stephenson as a token of respect and gratitude for his many contributions to railway engineering. The platforms and rails were boarded over and colourful drapes hung from the roof, busts of various worthies were lined along one side, and on the other, three enormous paintings of Stephenson's major works were hung. These have long since disappeared but the station continues in use with few alterations and is undoubtedly still one of the finest in the country.

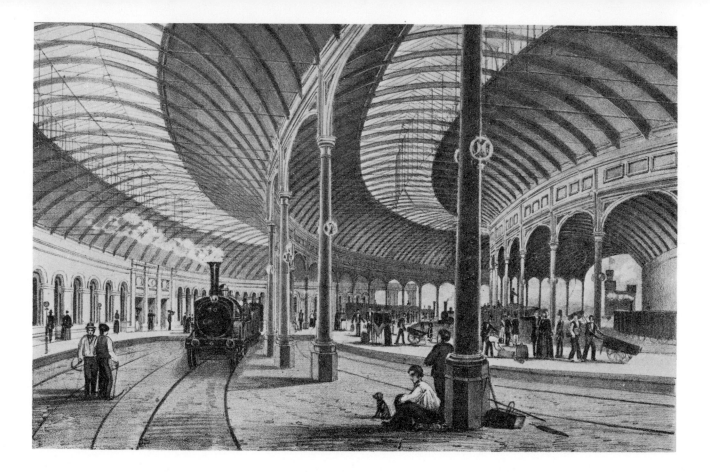

Newport, Abergavenny and Hereford Railway, extension to Taff Vale
Crumlin viaduct

Lettered with title and Mr Charles Liddell, engineer. Lithographed & published by Newman & Co. 48, Watling St., London.
Lithograph, coloured by hand
$11\frac{3}{8}$ in × $17\frac{1}{2}$ in (29·1 cm × 44·3 cm)

Few engineering feats in the nineteenth century could compare with that of T. W. Kennard in building the Crumlin viaduct. One third of a mile in length and almost two hundred feet high, it was designed to create a means of communication with the rich mineral districts of Monmouthshire and Glamorgan. The portion of the railway from Pontypool to the east side of the valley at Crumlin was opened on 20 August 1855. Many of the piers and cross girders of the viaduct, some of which were one hundred and fifty feet long and weighed fifty tons, were completed at that time but it was not finally opened until June 1857 after thorough tests on the strength and stability had been carried out. The remainder of the railway to Quaker's Yard, Taff Vale, was completed in January of the following year.

The Newport, Abergavenny and Hereford became part of the West Midland Railway in 1860 and that in turn was absorbed by the Great Western in the same year. The Crumlin viaduct was dismantled quite recently.

Cornwall Railway
Royal Albert Bridge at Saltash

Lettered with details of the construction and To the Directors of the Cornwall & South Devon Railways this view of the Royal Albert Bridge at Saltash, constructed of wrought iron, from the designs of I. K. Brunel, Esqre. F.R.S. is most respectfully inscribed by the Publisher. From a drawing by C. A. Scott, on stone by J. Needham. Day & Son Lithrs. to the Queen. Published by J. Heydon, Fore St. Devonport.
Lithograph, coloured by hand
11 in × 16⅜ in (28·1 cm × 41·5 cm)

Few railways were situated in more picturesque scenery than the Cornwall, and views from the train were enhanced by the fact that relatively few deep cuttings were made and most of the line was constructed on embankments and viaducts. The first sod had been cut, 'in spiritless manner', near Truro in August 1847, but work stopped almost immediately because of a depression and did not begin again until 1852, by which time it had been decided to abandon many of the branch lines which had initially been proposed. The most important engineering work associated with the new line was undoubtedly the Royal Albert bridge across the Tamar at Saltash, designed by Brunel, and opened by the Prince Consort in May 1859. Brunel's first designs had been for a timber structure of seven arches, but like Stephenson's first design for the Britannia bridge over the Menai Straits, this was rejected by the Admiralty on the grounds that it impaired navigation of the river. The bridge as built combines arch and suspension principles, the outward thrust of the tubular arches countering the inward drag of the suspension cables. It is undoubtedly one of the greatest surviving monuments to Brunel's genius, and it was appropriate that, even though the construction of his colossal iron ship the 'Great Eastern' had made him so ill that he could neither walk nor stand, he was drawn slowly over the completed bridge, on a flat truck, just a few weeks before his death on 15 September 1859.

Turin and Genoa Railway, Italy
Bridge over the River Scrivia at Prarolo

Lettered with title in Italian and C. Bossoli, del.. E. Walker, lith. Day & Son Lithrs to the Queen, London.
Colour lithograph
12 in × 17¼ in (30·3 cm × 44·1 cm)

Count Cavour, the liberal and progressive chief minister of Victor Emmanuel, King of Sardinia and Piedmont, realised that the railway could play an important part in assuring Italy's future by not only assisting in the unification of the states but also in facilitating the rapid transport of troops and arms against foreign invaders. Finding neither sufficient money, nor the expert knowledge to construct a railway, in Italy, he turned to England and to Thomas Brassey to help him. Brassey, who was probably the largest railway contractor in the world at that time, was sympathetic to Cavour's aims, and in 1853 signed a contract binding him to build a line from Turin to Novara a distance of sixty miles. The cost of building the railway proved far less than the original estimate, and it was so great a success that Brassey was employed to build several further lines. These included the Turin and Susa railway, over a distance of thirty-four miles, and the Ivrea branch, nineteen miles long. They culminated in the Victor Emmanuel Railway running seventy-three miles from the Alps on the west side of the Mont Cenis pass through Chambrey to Culoz on the Rhone, the then Franco-Italian frontier. When combined with his earlier work this meant that Brassey had built a continuous line connecting the Austrian and French frontiers.

These railways involved many steep gradients and it was thought at first that they would have to be worked with stationary engines, but the Italians eventually succeeded in working them with steam locomotives placed back to back.

Metropolitan Railway
Baker Street station

Lettered with title and Kell Bros. Chromo litho, Castle St., Holborn.
Chromolithograph
15 in × 23½ in (38 cm × 59·1 cm)

The Metropolitan Railway which connected Paddington, Baker Street, Euston, Kings Cross, and terminated at Farrington Street, was opened on 10 January 1863. Although mixed track had been laid, it was initially worked by the Great Western Railway using broad gauge rolling stock, but, when the Great Northern Railway, which also used part of the line, offered to open a service of its own, the Great Western took umbrage and threatened to withdraw completely. Myles Fenton, the General Manager of the Metropolitan, sought the assistance of the Great Northern, and the London and North Western, and succeeded in obtaining enough narrow gauge stock to operate the complete line independently of the Great Western, and consequently the latter withdrew, and the broad gauge track was taken up. In 1884, when the line from Aldgate to the Mansion House was opened, the Metropolitan became part of the Inner Circle.

The Metropolitan, London's first underground railway, was not constructed in a tunnel but was built for the most part in cuttings which were afterwards roofed in where convenient. Consequently there were a considerable number of short tunnels but the trains ran at frequent intervals above ground. One problem of locomotive construction on the line was that the engines should not emit smoke, and, until electrification early in the present century, they were often fitted with condensers. These caused considerable trouble and one of the Great Northern engines is recorded to have blown its dome off while standing in Bishops Road station.

Much of the original construction of the Metropolitan is still evident at Baker Street, Paddington and other stations on the Circle line.

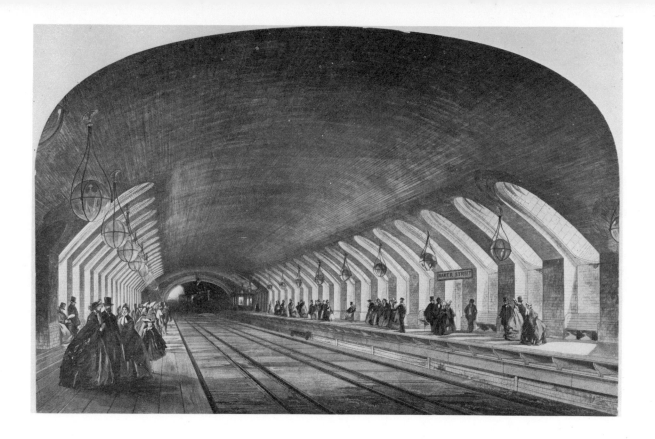

HER MAJESTY'S STATIONERY OFFICE

Government Bookshops

49 High Holborn, London WC1V 6HB
13a Castle Street, Edinburgh EH2 3AR
41 The Hayes, Cardiff CF1 1JW
Brazennose Street, Manchester M60 8AS
Southey House, Wine Street, Bristol BS1 2BQ
258 Broad Street, Birmingham B1 2HE
80 Chichester Street, Belfast BT1 4JY

*Government Publications are also available
through booksellers*

The full range of Museum publications
is displayed and sold at
The Victoria & Albert Museum
London SW7 2RL

Obtainable in the United States of America from
Pendragon House Inc.
2595 East Bayshore Road
Palo Alto
California 94303

Printed in England for Her Majesty's Stationery Office
by Product Support (Graphics) Limited, Derby
Dd 587541   K48